ON THE TRAIL TO
WOUNDED KNEE

To my grandmother Françoise.
Guy Le Querrec

Thanks to:

Robert Labatte and the Cheyenne River Cultural Center
Dave Bald Eagle and his family
Sara Remke
François Paolini
Joe Geshick
The residents of the Standing Rock, Cheyenne River, and Pine Ridge reservations who provided
help and hospitality and the Indian riders and horses, along with their friendly dog.

And friendly greetings to:

Valérie Crinière
Dave Hunt
Vincent Bidaut
and Tony Hymas, companion on the first journey.

The photographs were printed by the Publimod'Photo laboratory (printer: Hervé Hudry)
and the Magnum Photos laboratory.

Guy Le Querrec's photographs were taken with Leica cameras, models M6 and R6,
with 28 mm and 180 mm lenses.

Kodak Tri X film

Photographs on pages 12 and 13 © Nebraska State Historical Society, Lincoln.

ON THE TRAIL TO
WOUNDED KNEE

PHOTOGRAPHS

GUY LE QUERREC

Magnum Photos

INTRODUCTION

JIM HARRISON

TEXT

JEAN ROCHARD

———

THE LYONS PRESS
Guilford, Connecticut

An imprint of The Globe Pequot Press

INTRODUCTION
BY JIM HARRISON

———

The last thing any American of conscience wants to think about is the Sioux. It's like forgetting you have elbows and then banging one painfully against a doorjamb. You are stopped in your tracks, and the rather nominal pain reminds you of more seriously painful events, when you broke your back or neck, for instance.

Of the more than five hundred Native American tribes, we have treated none as badly as the Sioux. Up until recently even educated historians tended to refer to the massacre at Wounded Knee as the "Battle of Wounded Knee," which is akin to referring to the Battle of Treblinka, or the Battle of Buchenwald, or our own Battle of My Lai. After the end of our "Indian Wars," which were mostly prolonged butchery, there was no Marshal Plan but the creation of the Bureau of Indian affairs, surely the most insidious bureaucracy in the history of our republic. To bring us from the general to the particular, I recall twenty years ago on the Navajo reservation where up Keams Canyon I watched barefoot crippled children playing in the snow, an incredible image. A scant week later at the Nebraska Historical Society I looked at photos taken immediately after the massacre of Wounded Knee. My single eye blurred a bit (I'm blind in the other) when I saw a photo of a gully full of dead children. It had been bitterly cold and it was as if the frozen limbs of the children had arranged themselves in awkward supplication to the mute heavens.

The Statue of Liberty, that frequently malevolent bitch, has an enormous tumor in her gut that has spread to her brain and eyes. With regard to the Native Americans she has Alzheimer's or mad cow disease and can't remember her past, and her blind eyes can't see the terrifying plight of most of the Indian tribes. Meanwhile she blows China and stomps Cuba to death, choosing to forget the Native cultures she has already destroyed.

What to do? Keep our mouths shut. Stop giving them corrupt advice. But first and foremost we must make reparations. We must honor hundreds of treaties we have made. We must give back as much land as is humanly possible. In the case of the Sioux we must give back at least three quarters of the immense Black Hills. We have made paltry offers akin to stealing someone's home and offering ten dollars for their loss. General Phillip Sheridan, the famous warrior of the Civil and Indian Wars, said that, "a reservation is a worthless piece of land surrounded by scoundrels." In the case of the Sioux we pushed them to and fro, stole the best and left them the worst, a land on which they cannot survive without our pathetic allowances.

I remember way back in high school when I was sixteen and deeply immersed in studying Indian cultures, asking my wise teacher why we were so generous with the German and Japanese after World War II and were so vicious and cheap with the Indians. The teacher, a survivor of a POW camp, said that if we were fair to the Indians it would be an admission of guilt that we don't have the character to make. I was stunned at the time and perhaps I still am.

Similar massacres in terms of dimension, the numbers of bodies, had taken place at Sand Creek in Eastern Colorado with the Cheyenne, and Bear Creek with the Shoshone where one of our soldiers had described the massacre as a "frolic." To know the true history of our own country can be difficult indeed, but most appear to carry the burden lightly. Our schoolbooks never clearly admit that we got off the boat and murdered a widely varied civilization, its five hundred segments often owning immense sophistication in terms of art and oral literature. Our weaponry included guns, starvation, and disease. The fuel of our conquest was greed. As Bertolt Brecht said, "Whom you would destroy, you first portray as savage."

Now anyone can say "that's history," and the procedures we used have been used historically on six of the seven continents (the Canadian decimation of the Eskimo luckily allows us to include the Arctic). One of the grandest illusions in America is that we are getting better and better. This notion is basically caused by our perversion of Calvinism wherein the reward of virtue is wealth, ergo, we are wealthy so we are virtuous. One American citizen, Bill Gates, is worth one hundred billion dollars while half the Navajo lack indoor plumbing, true also of many of the Sioux. Shannon County, the home of Pine Ridge and the site of Wounded Knee, is the poorest county in the United States.

Winston Churchill once said that America usually does the right thing after it has exhausted the alternatives. Sadly, in the case of the Native Americans, Churchill was wrong. All of this is both widely known and widely ignored by intelligent people and politicians, not the same thing as everyone knows.

I find somewhat ironic that a Frenchman took the finest and truest photos I have ever seen of American Indians. Guy Le Querrec has the beautiful but ruthless eye of a tragedian. The Big Foot Memorial Ride to commemorate the hundredth anniversary of Wounded Knee took place in the bitterest December weather possible, below zero for days on end. Despite the terrifying cold these photos will start a fire in your brain that will last forever, assuming you are a true human being. It remains to be seen in America if we are collectively human beings. The soul of our nation is doomed until we act with honor on this matter.

Chronology

1492

Christopher Columbus lands
in San Salvador. He calls the inhabitants
"In Dio" ("those who belong to God").
The Spaniards begin the military conquest
of South and Central America.

1607

The English land in Virginia.
At first, they settle peaceably, then
they begin to drive Indian tribes away.
The Powhatans are decimated.
The Dutch and the French also
establish settlements.

1675

The Wampanoags and Narragansetts
are exterminated, inaugurating a long
and debilitating series of wars in which
such Indian leaders as Pontiac, Tecumseh,
and Black Hawk achieve fame.
These wars are often caught up
with battles among the French,
the British, and the American rebels.

1776

The United States of America declares
independence. Indian wars continue.
Many Eastern tribes are eradicated,
deported, or confined on small
reservations.

1829

Land west of the Mississippi is declared
Indian territory. But the discovery
of gold in California in 1848 leads to many
expeditions against tribes inhabiting
the territory.

1850

There is war against the Navajos
and the Apaches in the West as
the frontier continues to advance from
the East. Abuses and massacres
of the Plains Indians begin: Cheyennes,
Comanches, Arapahos, and Lakota Sioux,
most of whom have never before
seen white men.

1867

The American army is defeated
at Fetterman by Red Cloud's Lakota
and their Cheyenne allies.

1868

The Treaty of Fort Laramie guarantees
substantial territory for the Sioux.
The discovery of gold in the Black Hills
leads to increased settlement by
pioneers in Indian territory, encouraged
by the government.

1875

The War Department orders all Sioux
onto the reservations and declares all
the others hostile. Red Cloud gives in.

1876

General Custer leads a campaign against
"hostile" Indians. He and the Seventh
Cavalry are defeated at Little Big Horn by
the Lakota of Sitting Bull and Crazy Horse
and their Cheyenne, Arapaho, and Santee
Sioux allies. But pioneer settlements are
irreversible. In order to end the costly
Indian Wars, the government inaugurates
a ruthless bison hunt, depriving
the Indians of their principal resource.

1889

In the West, a Paiute named Wovoka
says he has had a vision: by dancing,
the Indians will make the white man
disappear and everything will be as it was.
This practice, the ghost dance, becomes
popular among many desperate tribes.

Three photographs taken by George Trager on January 1, 1891. Deaths among the Indians are estimated to have been 350. The twenty-five soldiers who died are thought to have been killed by machine-gun fire from their own regiment. Three days after the massacre, waiting for the blizzard to end, a detachment of soldiers returned to Wounded Knee to bury the frozen Indian corpses in a mass grave. The soldiers collected a plentiful supply of "souvenirs" from the bodies. The photograph of Big Foot (whose real name was Spotted Elk; Big Foot was the name given him by American soldiers) lying in the snow is an enduring symbol of the end of the Indian Wars.

1890

In October, two Lakota, Short Bull and Kicking Bear, return from Nevada with word of this new movement. Sitting Bull is keenly interested and sees in it a new possibility for resistance. The ghost dance spreads to the Standing Rock and Cheyenne River reservations. The Indians dance, troubling the US government, which sees it as a plot by Sitting Bull.

December 15, 1890

Sitting Bull is killed while being arrested on government orders. The Sioux do not retaliate because of this new nonviolent belief. They flee.

December 17, 1890

The members of Sitting Bull's tribe reach Big Foot's camp. When this disciple of the ghost dance learns of Sitting Bull's killing, he decides to lead his people to Pine Ridge to ask for help from Red Cloud. On the same day the War Department orders Big Foot's arrest. Big Foot comes down with pneumonia. The winter is harsh, and the mass of Sioux on the march is made up primarily of women and children, who are destitute.

December 28, 1890

Big Foot's people are intercepted at Porcupine by the Seventh Cavalry and taken to Wounded Knee.

December 29, 1890

Soldiers surround Big Foot's camp and open fire with a new model Hotchkiss machine gun. More than three hundred men, women, and children are massacred. Official history calls this massacre a "battle," after the award of thirty-four military medals.

1968

After many decades of denial of rights and attempts to eliminate the Indian (acculturation, sterilization of women, prohibition of religious practices, and the like), Indian demands come out into the open. The American Indian Movement is founded.

1973

Siege of Wounded Knee, bringing the American Indian Movement into conflict with the forces of the FBI.

1986

The vision of a medicine man leads the Lakota to follow the trail of their ancestors and to repeat Big Foot's journey.

December 15–29, 1990

Last ride on Big Foot's trail, a century after the massacre of Wounded Knee and the murder of Sitting Bull. The Lakota are led by Arvol Looking Horse.

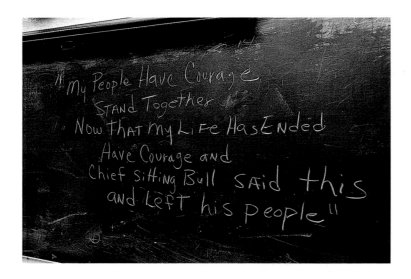

Guy Le Querrec and Jean Rochard met
in 1981. The idea for this photographic
report arose in 1989, during the recording
of the last piece on the record Oyate,
dedicated to Sitting Bull. With the English
composer Tony Hymas, Robert Labatte,
head of the Cheyenne River Cultural
Center, and two singers, Oley Little Eagle
and George Archambault, they went
to the school in Little Eagle.
On the blackboard was written:
"My people have courage.
Stand together. Now that my life
has ended, have courage,
and Chief Sitting Bull said this
and left his people." The next day,
George Archambault and Robert Labatte
took them to Sitting Bull's grave,
and they talked of the Big Foot Memorial
Ride. Guy Le Querrec and Jean Rochard
decided to return. Robert was
their invaluable traveling companion.

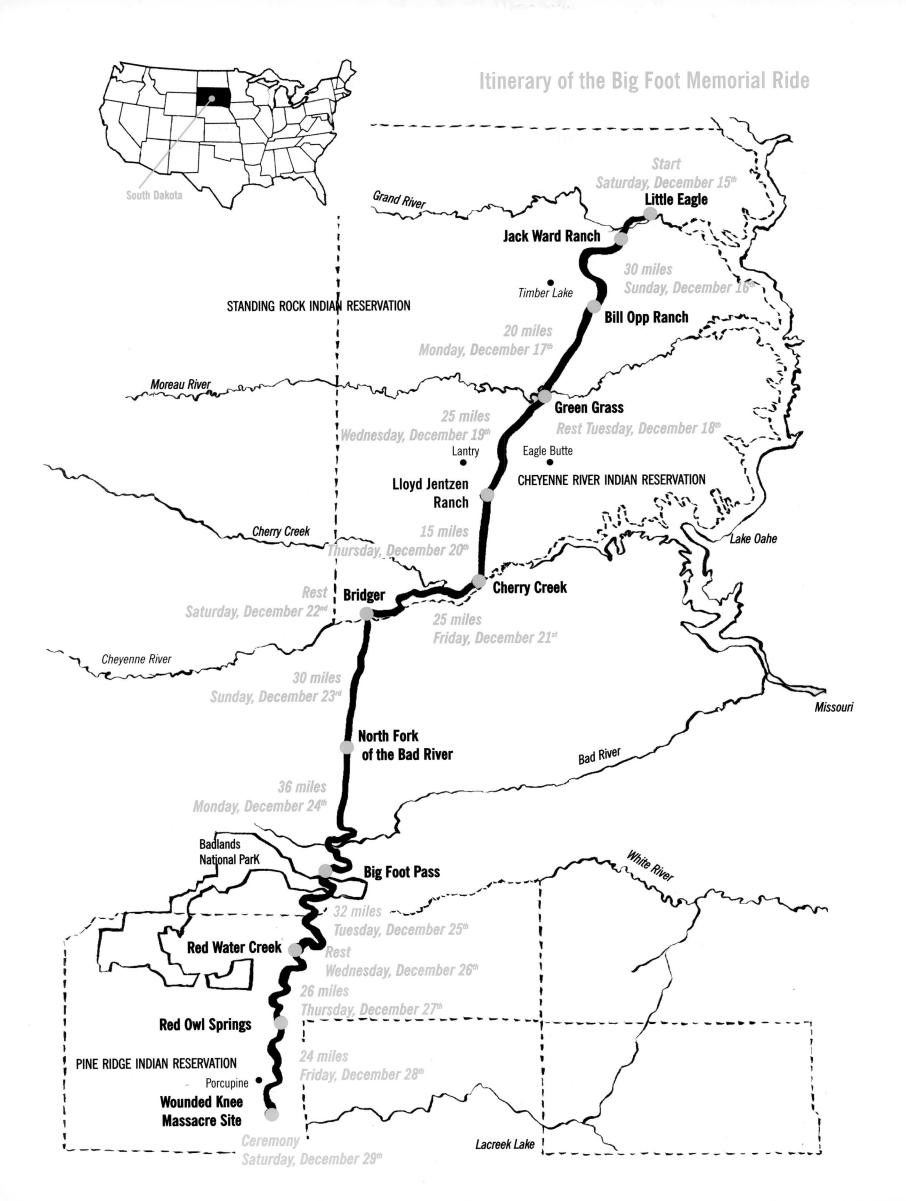

Itinerary of the Big Foot Memorial Ride

South Dakota

Grand River

Start
Saturday, December 15th
Little Eagle

Jack Ward Ranch

30 miles
Sunday, December 16th

Timber Lake

Bill Opp Ranch

STANDING ROCK INDIAN RESERVATION

20 miles
Monday, December 17th

Moreau River

Green Grass

25 miles
Wednesday, December 19th

Rest Tuesday, December 18th

Lantry

Eagle Butte

CHEYENNE RIVER INDIAN RESERVATION

Lloyd Jentzen Ranch

Cherry Creek

Lake Oahe

15 miles
Thursday, December 20th

Rest
Saturday, December 22nd

Bridger

Cherry Creek

25 miles
Friday, December 21st

Missouri

Cheyenne River

30 miles
Sunday, December 23rd

North Fork of the Bad River

Bad River

36 miles
Monday, December 24th

Badlands National Park

Big Foot Pass

White River

32 miles
Tuesday, December 25th

Red Water Creek

Rest
Wednesday, December 26th

26 miles
Thursday, December 27th

Red Owl Springs

PINE RIDGE INDIAN RESERVATION

Porcupine

24 miles
Friday, December 28th

Wounded Knee Massacre Site

Ceremony
Saturday, December 29th

Lacreek Lake

Sunday, December 16, 1990

"Follow your path my child, follow your path my child, and you will become a nation," a few undaunted survivors chanted in the wake of the Wounded Knee massacre. It was said then that the seventh generation born after Wounded Knee would restore unity to the Lakota people. One hundred years later the horsemen of Standing Rock and Cheyenne River reservations set off again on the path of their ancestors. Among them were children of that seventh generation.

At the age of twelve, Arvol Looking Horse (center, wearing a hat, preceding photograph), who was born in 1954, became the guardian of the sacred pipe, a symbol of unity, for which his family has been responsible for nineteen generations. In 1986, after the vision of a medicine man, he and some other spiritual leaders initiated the Big Foot Ride, commemorating the prophecy of the "restoration of the sacred circle of the Lakota nation." The last ride in the sequence would take place in 1990, one hundred years after the massacre. The youngest of the riders, Josh Guerrero, age seven, covered the entire distance on his pony.

Every day, before leaving, the circle was formed. It grew larger every day. That morning, as Arvol Looking Horse was praying with an old woman of the tribe, Guy entered the circle.

He was immediately waved out. Later in the day, some Indian riders explained the importance of the circle to him.

Ron McNeil, as Sitting Bull, like him
comes from Little Eagle in Standing Rock
reservation where Sitting Bull had also
lived. Throughout the journey, he was
an indomitable rider.

After the murder of Sitting Bull
on December 15, 1890,
one of his supporters, the Hunkpapa Crow
Woman, confronted the Indian police
and the soldiers. He was wearing a ghost
shirt and began to chant: *"Father.
I thought you had said that we were
all going to live again."* The soldiers fired,
but Crow Woman managed to escape.

At night around the fire, some surprising
questions delicately asked, raise
the matter of our responsibility
as Europeans. *"Suppose we sent
them back; what would you do with
them?"* asked an old man. A younger man
wearing an old patch from the seventies:
"US out of North America," asked:
*"And how did your de Gaulle get
rid of them?"*

The bison was everything for the Plains
Indians. In summer, the tribes carried
out large group hunts providing food
and furs for the entire winter.
Seeing no way out of the costly Indian
Wars, the American government wore
out Indian resistance through
the elimination of the bison.
While the riders rested, Robert Labatte
took us to the east of the Cheyenne River
reservation where bison are once again
being raised. As we stopped before
a dead bison, an eagle hovered above us.
Of all birds, the eagle is the one who flies
highest and sees everything.
Robert was very moved.

A little further on, an immense automobile graveyard. Accidents are frequent, often caused by alcoholic despair. *"Alcoholism, unemployment close to ninety per cent here, and negative things come from the lack of a reason for living. Riders who have participated in this journey will return home with a new reason for living."* This is the hope of Ron McNeil.

The day before, the tribal council
of Cheyenne River had offered a bison
and a thousand dollars to the riders,
provided they changed course and went
through Eagle Butte, the chief town
on the reservation. After a long discussion
in which all points of view were calmly
expressed until consensus was reached,
the decision was made to refuse.
"Our ancestors did not have that!"
"We're not in a parade." The horses did
not go through Eagle Butte, but the riders
went there on foot or by car for the evening
meeting. Political organization
on reservations is complex, and there
are many conflicts between tribal councils
and traditionalist or separatist Indians,
with the latter often thinking that the
former are manipulated by the Bureau
of Indian Affairs in Washington.

Arvol Looking Horse speaks to the riders
and their companions at the cultural
center in Eagle Butte. That night
he alluded to the impending American
intervention in Iraq. Above him
is a painting of Big Foot, lying dead
in the snow, and small pennants recalling
the seven Lakota groups: Minnecoju,
Oglala, Two Kettle (Oohenonpa), Blackfoot

(Sihasapa), Sans-Arc (Itazipco),
Brulé (Sichango), Hunkpapa.
Sioux is a generic term for the Dakota,
Nakota, and Lakota invented by French
trappers. They had partially retained
the mocking nickname given them
by the neighboring Chippewa,
"Nadwessiou" (crawling snake).

We headed for the gymnasium,
where a ceremony was being held.
At that point, we were no longer filming
or taking photographs. Our friend
Robert Labatte, wrapped in a bison skin,
received his Lakota name: Wablaza,

"he who sees high." Now we understood
his feeling on seeing the eagle
that morning. This was followed
by the first powwow, bringing together
singers and dancers from the area.
The children were free and happy.

Green Grass is a place full of history
and ghosts. The sweat lodge is a place
for spiritual, mental, and physical
purification. Water is poured on heated
stones, creating dense vapor for
the participants seated in a circle around
the stones. This ceremony, long
interpreted as a threat to government
power, precedes or accompanies all rituals
and events in the life of the reservation;
and the day before this, the ceremony
of the riders.

It was at Green Grass that Crazy Horse
participated in the sun dance before
the battle of Little Big Horn, and there
the sacred pipe of unity is kept.
That morning, there was a particular
feeling caught by the blizzard.
The temperature fell below minus 50.

Little Josh's grandmother drives the food wagon. Women of various generations surround the riders with much care and devotion.

In 1519, Hernando Cortés began the conquest of Mexico. In less than three years, he crushed the Aztec empire. He had sixteen horsemen with him. This was the first appearance of horses on American soil.

The animal reached North America,
where it held great attraction for many
Plains tribes, Comanche, Kiowa, Sioux,
Cheyenne. They were so fond of it that
they cross-bred it passionately, creating
new species of horse. This was the only
truly loving encounter with an element
from the European onslaught.

The cold was unbearable.
In the evening, when, like all
the participants, Guy introduced himself,
he was warmly applauded by the riders
when he said to them: *"My English is
very weak, but I have learned two words:
cold and courage."*

Thursday, December 20, 1990   Throughout the entire journey,
Arvol Looking Horse and Ron McNeil,
present from the beginning, did not
leave the front rank of riders.

Friday, December 21, 1990
The irony of clichés, some frozen blue
jeans, a herd of cattle. Often, in order
to work, good Indian riders have to become
good cowboys.

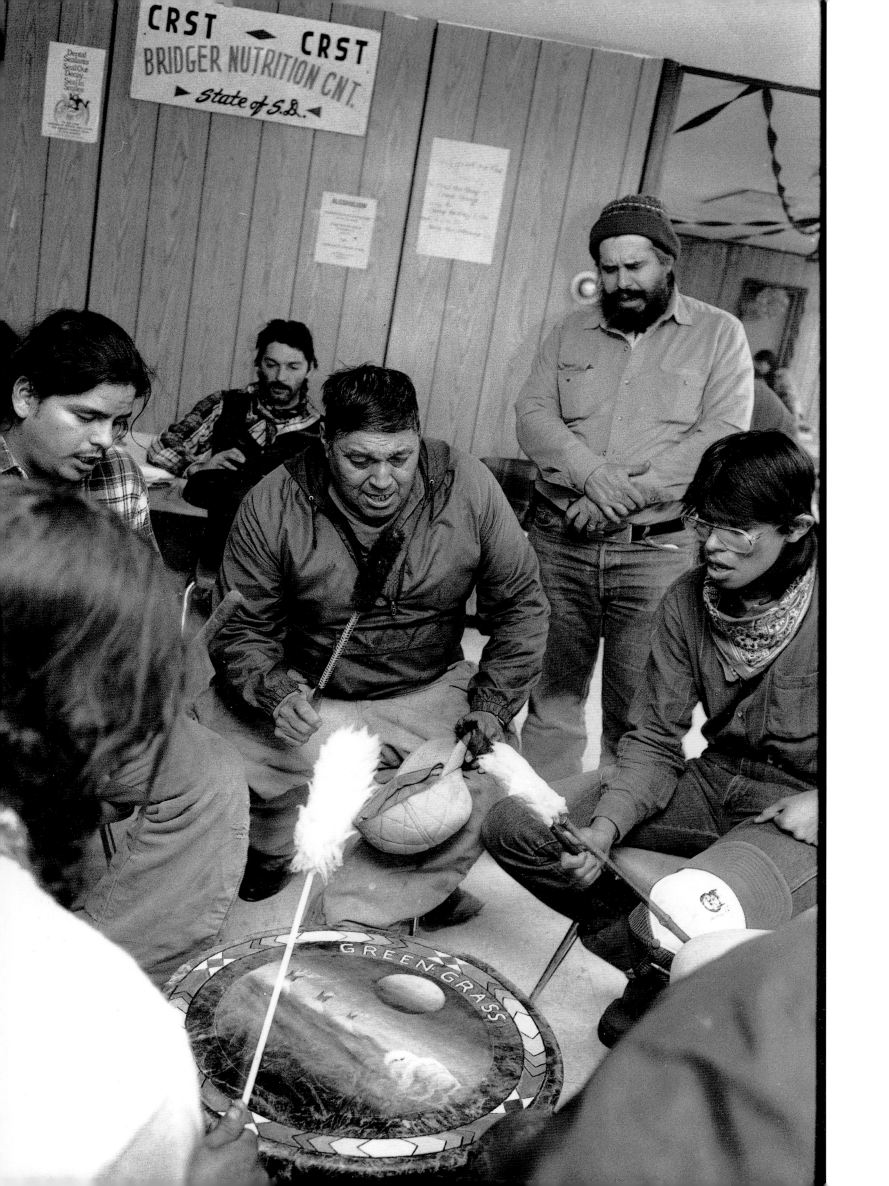

At the Nutrition Center in Bridger,
reputedly the poorest place
in the United States, they sing before
the next day's meeting.

Saturday, December 22, 1990

Seeing our curiosity about the American flag hanging in the Bridger community room, an old man whispered to us: *"It's ours; we took it from them at Little Big Horn."* Riders came in from all sides. The thirty or so riders from Standing Rock and Cheyenne River were swelled by Lakota from the neighboring reservations of Lower Brulé, Crow Creek, Rosebud, and Pine Ridge, and Indians from other tribes, Chippewa, Choctaw, and even a Micmac from Canada joined them, reminding us that the history of American colonialism was not confined to the tragic defeat of the Sioux. In the Bridger gymnasium, the circle is formed with the new arrivals. They say prayers for the second part of the journey.

Big Foot Memorial Ride

Sunday, December 23, 1990 Crossing the frozen Cheyenne River
(following pages), given that name in 1860
by a group of soldiers who had seen
a group of Cheyenne camp there.

The map of the United States bears
so many mistaken signs, names of Indian
origin, misunderstandings, that are all
so many graves.

"Who thinks that you have come?
Who thinks that you have come?
Is it someone looking for his mother?
Is it someone looking for his mother?"
— Ghost dance song of 1890

Every day, we heard about the Black Hills
(Paha Sapa). In 1868, the Treaty of Fort
Laramie guaranteed a reservation
to the Lakota covering more than half
of South Dakota, and parts of Montana,

Wyoming, and North Dakota.
The discovery of gold in the Black Hills
provoked a rush and the violation
of existing treaties.

The demand for restitution
of the Black Hills remains central today.
There are more than three hundred treaties
in force between the various reservations
in the United States and the government,
which are not always respected.

Coming around a hill, a scene briefly
evokes a celebrated photograph out
of the past, a picture by Edward Sheriff
Curtis, the most famous of all
the photographers of Indians. His first
photograph dates from 1895, five years
after the massacre. Until his death
in 1930, he unceasingly documented what
he called "the vanishing race."
His pictures, like those of William Henry
Jackson, Frank Jay Haynes, and Laton
A. Huffman, told a more accurate story
about the Indians than a century
of cinema, in turn propagandist, vengeful,
lying, brutal, coarse, paternalistic,
and humanistic.

"My children, my children,
Look! The earth is starting to move,
Look! The earth is starting to move,
My father tells me so,
My father tells me so."
—Ghost dance song of 1890

Somewhere in the Badlands—a rocky lunar landscape north of the Pine Ridge reservation—buried in a secret place lies the body of Crazy Horse, emblematic leader, victor at Little Big Horn, murdered in prison. Crazy Horse had always refused to be photographed. The ghost dancers of 1890 hoped through their dance to restore to life this mythic warrior without an image and without a grave.

On the evening of December 24, 1890,
Big Foot's small troop stopped at the door
of a church, asking for help from a group
of Christians who had come together
for midnight mass. They were driven off;
the memory remains.

Wednesday, December 26, 1990   While the riders rested, a Lakota insisted
that we go to his uncle's house.
The uncle's name is Eli Tail, and he has
appeared several times at the United
Nations to argue for Indian rights.
*"Crazy Horse and Sitting Bull fought
very hard for our land. We are still
here today and it is up to us to fight for
our children, or else the United States
will eliminate us for good."*

Thursday, December 27, 1990

Birgil Kills Straight, an Oglala from
Pine Ridge and a member of the Indigenous
Law Institute, is one of the most active
figures both in the reservation and
in relations with the outside world.
Kills Straight, Looking Horse, Not Help Him,
Bald Eagle, Red Cloud...

Following Wounded Knee, all Indians
were supposed to have European style
surnames. This was the end of names
that changed with age. Some names were
Anglicized, some were given the names
of French trappers, or had English names
listed on a board forced on them.

Crooks and staffs with eagle
feathers indicate the leaders
of the moment. Each feather is earned
by a beneficent action.

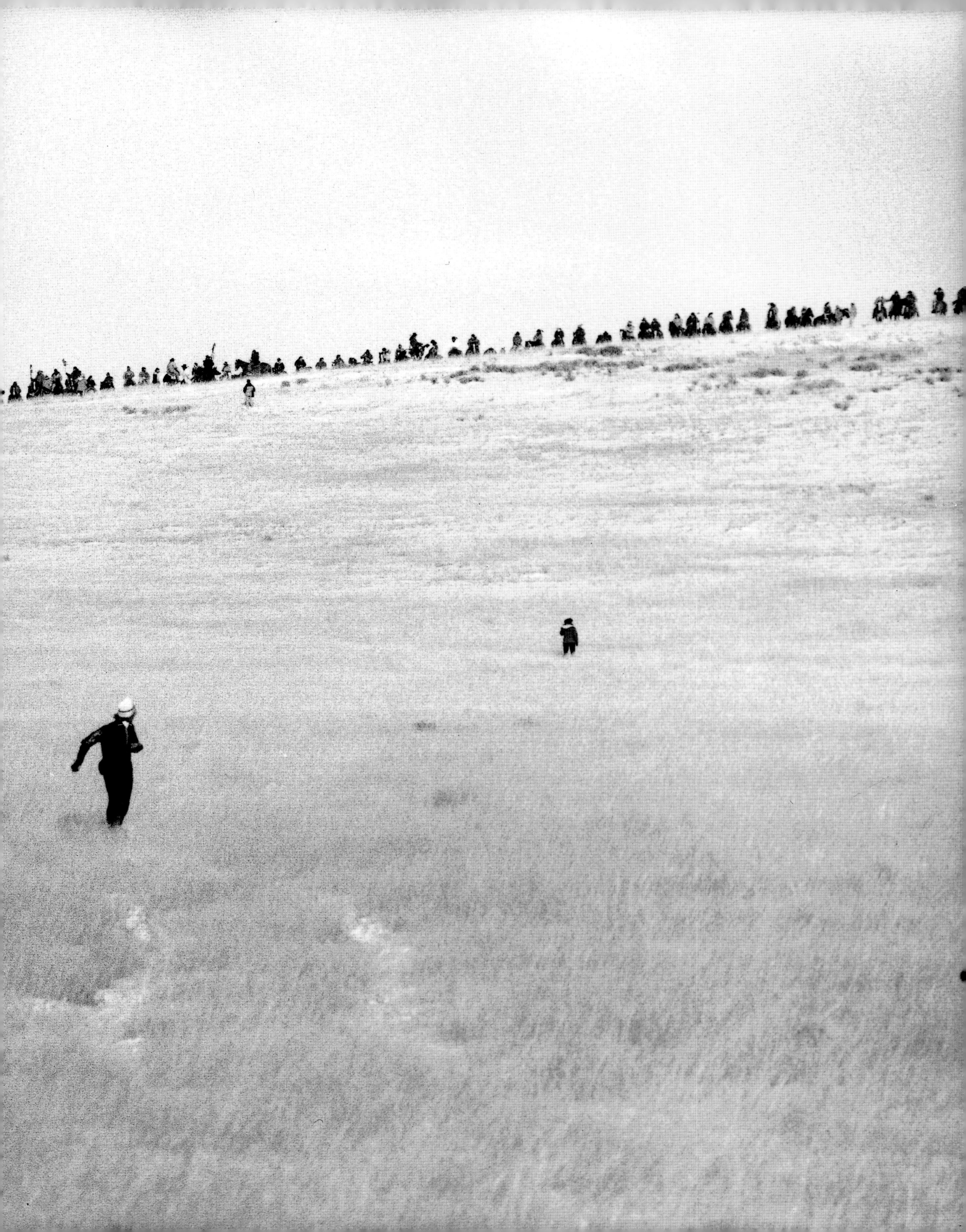

Friday, December 28, 1990

On December 28, 1890, four groups
of the Seventh Cavalry, the regiment
defeated at Little Big Horn, surrounded Big
Foot's troop at Porcupine. Big Foot,
ill and spitting blood, appeared before
Major Whiteside with a white flag.

The soldier informed him that he had
been ordered to arrest him
as a troublemaker and demanded that
all the men be disarmed and dismounted.
The soldiers conducted the Indians
to Wounded Knee.

An AIM (American Indian Movement) flag reminds us of another event at Wounded Knee: the siege of 1973 opposing the new Indian resistance to the troops of the FBI. From time to time, we heard the name of Leonard Peltier, a Lakota and the longest held known political prisoner on the planet.

*"The reconstruction of the Sioux nation
by the seventh generation will become
a reality. This is the beginning,"*
confides Ron McNeil.

In the gymnasium in Wounded Knee,
on the basketball court (a very popular
game among Indian tribes), Josh Guerrero
receives an eagle feather, sign
of his bravery. A symbol of the seventh
generation, he accomplished the entire
Big Foot Ride from Little Eagle to Wounded
Knee on his pony.

In community rooms, signs conflict:
crucifixes and Bibles against eagle feathers.

The powwow that evening strongly evokes other times and other hopes, when the dance was supposed to bring about unity. There we meet Eli Tail again. He tells us that he is also dancing for the children.

"I look to the future for the benefit of my children. And that is what I mean when I say that you should take good care of this land for me."
—Sitting Bull, August 1883

Saturday, December 29, 1990

At dawn on December 29, 1890, the camp was surrounded by Hotchkiss machine guns. The remnant of the Seventh Cavalry had come as reinforcements. Colonel James W. Forsyth took charge of operations. Some soldiers were already celebrating the capture of Big Foot with whiskey. The soldiers went into the tents and brought back knives, tent poles, rifles, and all bundles, which they ripped open. Then they ordered the Indians to take off loin cloths and blankets. Yellow Bird protested and danced. Only two Indians still had rifles. One of them brandished his. The soldiers opened fire with deadly fury, even killing twenty-five of their own men. On the Indian side, four men and forty-seven women and children survived. One hundred years later, on the coldest day, the tears are dried. Big Foot and some three hundred other Lakota were buried in a mass grave in the cemetery in Wounded Knee.

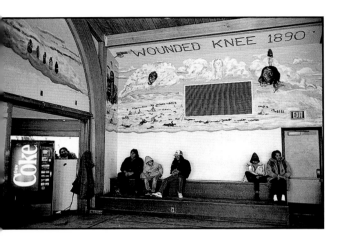

"Every time you see the photo of Big Foot
lying dead in the snow, it sends you back
to 1890, to what happened here;
it also sends you back a little later
to the 1970s when something happened;
it sends you back to yesterday, to today;
it's a form of unity. Every time that unity is
on the point of being recovered,
we must be very cautious: when the ghost
dance restored hope and unity,
it was crushed at Wounded Knee."
Mary Not Help Him, descendant of Dewey
Beard, survivor of Wounded Knee
and warrior at Little Big Horn.